Believe in Yourself
Mental Strength

By Cathy Wilson

Copyright © 2014

Copyright © 2014 by Cathy Wilson

ISBN-13:
978-1503239685

ISBN-10:
1503239683

All Rights Reserved. No part of this publication may be reproduced in any form or by any means, including scanning, photocopying, or otherwise without prior written permission of the copyright holder.

First Printing, 2014

Printed in the United States of America

Income Disclaimer

This book contains business strategies, marketing methods and other business advice that, regardless of my own results and experience, may not produce the same results (or any results) for you. I make absolutely no guarantee, expressed or implied, that by following the advice below you will make any money or improve current profits, as there are several factors and variables that come into play regarding any given business.

Primarily, results will depend on the nature of the product or business model, the conditions of the marketplace, the experience of the individual, and situations and elements that are beyond your control.

As with any business endeavor, you assume all risk related to investment and money based on your own discretion and at your own potential expense.

Liability Disclaimer

By reading this book, you assume all risks associated with using the advice given below, with a full understanding that you, solely, are responsible for anything that may occur as a result of putting this information into action in any way, and regardless of your interpretation of the advice.

You further agree that our company cannot be held responsible in any way for the success or failure of your business as a result of the information presented in this book. It is your responsibility to conduct your own due diligence regarding the safe and successful operation of your business if you intend to apply any of our information in any way to your business operations.

Terms of Use

You are given a non-transferable, "personal use" license to this book. You cannot distribute it or share it with other individuals.

Also, there are no resale rights or private label rights granted when purchasing this book. In other words, it's for your own personal use only.

Believe in Yourself
Mental Strength
By Cathy Wilson

Table of Contents

Introduction 9

Better Mental: Open Your Mind to Change 11

Improved Physical..25

Nutritional Improvement 31

Emotional Wellness...37

Elite Social 41

Sound Spiritual..49

Final Thoughts . . . Better Life, Better You 53

Introduction

If you want to be genuinely happy, you're going to have to learn to love yourself first. You are no good to anyone else if you can't **CHOOSE** to put yourself first. This doesn't mean you disregard all thoughts, feelings, and actions of others. There's a fine line here.

Putting yourself first is the only way you are going to reach your true potential in love, life, and happiness. Being the best that you can be is the first stepping stone. **Believe** from here it only gets better.

Better Cognitive . . .

Improved Physical . . .

Smart Nutrition Choices . . .

Emotional Wellness. . .

Elite Social . . .

Satisfying Spiritual . . .

Sensational Life . . .

Better You!

So where does it start? Well it starts in your head, with your mental. The mind is a powerful thing. Tapping into it positively is going to change your life for the better. Mind over matter you might say. Think it, believe it, and it will become your reality. The most important concept we all need to understand is that, **"You Are In Charge Of You!"**

Your life is a result of the decisions you've made. Some are controllable and others aren't, but regardless, they are your decisions. We often make excuses in failure. Blaming others when we fail. We even make excuses to make excuses when we don't end up with the results we wanted or expected.

By taking responsibility for your actions, and stepping up to the plate so to speak. By understanding, believing, and utilizing the power of your mind, you can make the decision to **Choose Yourself First Today,** and start living the life you have always dreamed of.

Better Mental: Open Your Mind to Change

"Change only happens with an open mind, where your thoughts and beliefs are the windows of the world. You've got to scrub them every once in a while, or you won't be able to see out." CAW

In order to open your mind to mental change, which is going to benefit you as a whole, you need to look or consider strategies to help you take care of, or better your thinking.

Here are a few basic tips and tricks to help you care for your mental health.

Open Up About Your Uninhibited Feelings

As humans, we need to release negative thoughts and feelings build up naturally over time. Many people for various reasons choose to keep their feelings bottled up inside, making a dangerous habit of this. Psychologists deem this very unhealthy and destructive. Experts agree it's important to talk regularly about your feelings, to express yourself in a neutral or positive view, in order to take charge of your well-being. This ensures you are doing what you can to stay healthy using you noggin first!

Action steps may be . . .

- Talking with a friend or family member

- Conversing with a stranger

- Talking to your pet or other animal friend

- Perhaps even venting to an object that comforts you or makes you feel secure

Extended Communication with Others

We have an internal need to feel wanted and loved unconditionally. In order to feel positive about ourselves, it's important we interact and are accepted by others. Taking the time to stay connected with friends and family is critical in any healthy individual.

Getting advice and tapping into the brain of another person will help you open your mind, and perhaps consider another angle or option that's been troubling you.

Connections with others keeps you active, grounded, and will help you find solutions to issues that you might otherwise stumble on with indefinitely.

Actions steps might be . . .

- Phoning up an old friend and going out for coffee

- Making the effort to attend family functions

- Scheduling regular holidays with friends throughout the year

- Picking up the phone and talking with loved ones on a routine basis

- Making the effort to find new friends regularly

- Blocking off time to spend with your immediate family

Pay Attention to Good Nutrition

Nutritional experts agree, what you eat and how you feel are dependent upon one another. The better you eat and the better you look physically, the more confident and positivite you will see in yourself. Of course there are always exceptions to the rules, but if your brain is wired "normally," eating well is only going to heighten positive perspective in everything.

Just consider for a minute how a cup of coffee makes you feel? It's good for a period of time right? Making a point of filling your body up with healthy and nutritious macronutrients, including lean meats, complex carbohydrates, and healthy fats, is going to get your mind headed in the right direction. Add to this the essential micronutrients required for good health, and you'll be well on your way to "Optimistic-ville."

Actions steps might be . . .

- Ensuring you eat a healthy breakfast of lean protein and good carbs, like a piece of whole grain toast with peanut butter before heading out the door.

- Choosing to snack on fruits, vegetables, and other nutritious snacks instead of candy bars and pastries, that are loaded with calories, bad fat, and other toxic chemicals.

- Drinking lots of pure water instead of sugar loaded sodas and juices.

- Eating regularly throughout the day to keep your blood sugars up, and your mood and mind level.

- Making sure you get adequate fuel into your body, so your mind has the energy to function, and your physical isn't screaming for food.

Learn to Love Yourself

This one can be extremely tough, but it is necessary if you're going to choose yourself first. Let me ask you something. If you don't love yourself, how can you expect anybody else to love you? Isn't that a huge part of being human? Finding people that love and validate you for you, so that you can find that internal happiness so critical to life?

Find what you are good at and do it! Perhaps you are a fabulous cook and love doing it. Showcase it by having friends and family over, so you can shine and feel fabulous about you. Psychologists agree, there are all sorts of different methods to help you let go of the negative, focus on the positive, and learn to love you.

Another method is to tell yourself something positive every single morning just after rising. Maybe you love your crazy long legs. Verbally tell yourself this each and every morning, so you give yourself the ability to actually enjoy and believe this fact. Never mind that you think your nose is too long, or your ears are too big. That really doesn't matter, because the best you can do with those factors is to accept them as they are and move on. Don't let what you don't "love," interfere with your enjoyment of what is fabulous about you. Makes sense right?

Actions steps might be . . .

- Having a journal beside your bed and writing something positive about yourself in it every single morning whether you are grumpy or not.

- Placing sticky notes throughout your house strategically of a positive quote or something that reminds you to smile.

Schedule Regular Timeouts

It's so very important to get into the habit of taking a step back every once in awhile to change your pace and reflect. You should make a point every day to take a five or ten minute break just for you. Maybe you want to read a book or do some stretches. It's also important to schedule longer breaks here and there. Perhaps you might like to go away for a week 2-3 times a year to escape. Or a weekend once a month to a quiet place in a tranquil setting works for you. It really doesn't matter where, just that you do it.

Actions steps might be . . .

- Having a set time each day where you take a walk around the block to clear your head.

- Scheduling a few trips each year where you get a change of scenery and no routine to enjoy.

- Planning a weekend away here and there to lose yourself in nothingness, or just do things you wouldn't normally.

Ask For Help

This is a tough one, because the dreaded ego often gets in the way. Scientists and psychologists alike dictate the ego often causes more issues than it's worth. But you better get used to it cuz you're stuck with it! Like myself, many people just have a tough time asking others for help. What you need to keep in mind, is you're not "Wonder-Woman" or "Superman." You can only do what you can do, and that doesn't include everything.

If you're tired, overwhelmed, or worried, give yourself permission to ask someone for help and follow through with it. Don't wait until you realize things are out of hand before you turn to someone. Proactive is a good thing here, and by asking for help when you need it, and even before, you're choosing yourself first. Understand you DESERVE to come first.

Actions steps might be . . .

- Maybe you have a bad cold and are trying to run your kids here, there, and everywhere, when you know a neighbor would be happy to scoot them around. Stop yourself and ask for help.

- At work you might be trying to "do it all" when you don't need to. Delegate and allow other people to do things you know they can get accomplished. Lessen your load, and give what you aren't very good at to others to get done. Ask for help and get less stressed because of this.

- Maybe you are planning on cleaning out your garage on the weekend. Ask a few friends to help you out. This way you are going to have a little fun and get the job done a heck of a lot faster. You deserve to have it easier than you do.

Stay Physically Fit

Health experts know when you get your heart rate pumping, endorphins are released from your brain that help you to feel good. This contributes to boosting self-confidence, bettering sleep, losing weight, and helping you to look and feel fabulous. Your body and brain work as a unit, and regular exercise is going to help keep them in sync and a gynormous smile upon your face.

Actions steps could be . . .

- Taking a nice brisk walk each day at lunch to get your body moving.

- Joining a gym and training 3-4 times a week.

- Attending aerobics or boot camp fitness classes regularly, that are going to help you meet great new friends while losing weight, and gaining the belief in yourself that you deserve.

- Take an hour each day to focus on a different fitness activity. It could be hiking, biking, tennis, skating, swimming, or any other physical activity that/s going to help you feel great inside and out.

Extend a Hand

Showing your caring factor is going to help you feel better about yourself. There's just something about helping others that truly makes us feel really good about ourselves. Whether it's just asking a friend if she wants you to grab her dry cleaning, or offering to run a few errands for someone. The idea is that you make an effort to help someone else and it will come back around.

Action steps may be . . .

- Getting groceries for an elderly person.

- Running errands for a friend.

- Offering to help a boy-toy with cleaning.

- Volunteering for a charity.

Do What You Love

It's really important to do things you love. Are you going to love everything you do? Of course not. But it's really important you make the time to do things that make you smile just for you.

Actions steps may be . . .

- Taking painting classes may be something you love doing. Take the time to put them into your schedule, because this is only going to help you relax and look for the good in yourself and life.

- Maybe going for a quiet swim in the lake is something that refreshes you.

- Think of things you might like to try and figure out a way to do them. Maybe you always wanted to learn to knit or take pole dancing classes.

Easy on the Alcohol

Having a glass of wine here and there is actually beneficial for your health, according to medical experts. The problems arise when people take advantage of this, and start using alcohol to cope with problems. Moderation is important and understanding the mood lifting effect of alcohol is temporary.

Action steps might be . . .

- Limiting yourself to one alcoholic beverage at dinner time.

- When you go out for the evening, volunteer to be the designated driver, so you don't even have the opportunity to drink too much.

- If you find that you are drinking too much, and it's interfering with your happiness, it's critical you get help.

* *The Power of Positive Thinking*

You are ultimately responsible for each of your life experiences, and it's key to note that how you think and perceive things, positively or negatively, have a direct effect on the outcome, whether you turn left or right in life, or run right through the stop sign.

Some people are conditioned to believe that life will decide their destiny and not themselves. That their actions and thoughts have zero to do with their experiences. That's a crock, and most expert professionals in the field of thinking and mind power agree.

YOU WILL BECOME WHAT YOU ARE THINKING, AND THESE THOUGHTS ARE WHAT WILL DETERMINE YOUR LIFE REALITY.

Science even stands behind this belief, suggesting by controlling and thinking good thoughts. it's possible to carve new pathways in your brain. Scientific study believes you can actually rewire the patterns in your brain with specific and continuous cognitive behavioral affirmations. This proves positive thinking can actually alter your brain wiring, triggering chemical affects, which changes your life in absolute.

This is an introductory book, and I don't want to get too deep here. But what you need to consider, is that you actually can alter your destiny by looking for and more importantly believing in the positive. Pretty powerful stuff don't you think?

So Where Does Your Unhappiness Come From?

Do you want it straight up or sugar coated? It comes directly from your unhappy or negative thought. If you have too much negative, you will create other mental issues for yourself like depression. Sadly, this illness often gets treated or handled with medications, which really are only a temporary fix masking the problem.

From there, you'll eventually trigger all sorts of other unhappy thoughts, influenced both by natural and unnatural means. This is one huge cycle that just keeps building, because the root of the problem is buried and never dealt with.

Instead of just focusing on the positive and making sure you skip past most of the negatives, you end up looking to blame your sadness on something else, and this just makes it that much harder to remove the negative interference, and make your reality a happy one.

When you're down, it's easy to get kicked, and this is when your ego dismisses the fact that something so trivial and easy as positive thought, could actually turn your world around for the better. Seems like a no-win situation, and that's usually how it stays.

Here are a few negative thoughts you can flip to positive, which will help you make your reality so much more than you ever dreamed. Believe it and it WILL become your reality.

You just don't have enough - It just doesn't make sense that you need to have certain things with your happiness comes from inside of you.

I will never be a pretty as other girls - You are pretty enough for you and the more you focus on taking care of yourself the prettier you will become.

It's probably never going to happen - It will happen, and if it doesn't you'll still be happy because the outcome will be better than if you never considered it.

I can't live without them - You loved and cared for them and are very hurt, but will heal in time and be stronger because of them.

I just don't have the gifts they have - I bet you'll be surprised what you can accomplish if you set your mind to it.

I am just too set in my ways to ever change – It's important to be strong in your beliefs, but you are also willing to change if you want. You are intelligent and can change if you'd like to.

* You need to believe in yourself and understand if you want to heal yourself and change your reality you can. You may think you're helpless and just stuck with what you are experiencing in the now, but this isn't true. You have the ultimate power of change, which is your mind, and if you consciously want to change your life for the better it starts with your thoughts.

My Thoughts . . .

If you are expecting to make positive changes for you, it's important to ensure you are doing everything in your power to open your mind to change, and release the negative that is causing interference in your happiness and wellbeing. Positive thinking is what will make your realities and life experiences what you want. And you need to understand, embrace, and accept this, looking to make change, believe and see it through to the end, or the beginning, depending on your perception.

When making the most of you, it's so very important for you to take action with your mental health, doing whatever you can to make your perception of YOU more productively positive.

Mind over matter is a very powerful concept.

Improved Physical

Experts agree, you attract people most like yourself. It's not just on the romantic and sexual platforms, but also the metaphysical and physical. Somehow "they" just seem to "show up." Your aura, natural chemicals, and internal energies just throw certain messages out into the universe, and this sways specific people to venture your way.

You have a unique belief system that identifies you, and your physical appearance is a part of this, or maybe it's better to say a reflection of. Fact is, the way people "see" you or perceive your physical, causes them to form an opinion, to turn left or right, or head straight toward you.

Each person is pre-programmed or interested in certain physical traits in another person whether it's learned or not, conscious or unconscious. Let's say a star basketball player on the girls' high school team is physically attracted to athletic, outgoing, and socially popular guys that play sports. Perhaps she is drawn to football or soccer players. The idea is that her blinders are pretty much up for antisocial computer nerds that lack confidence and only get excited when extra homework is assigned.

This girl pays attention to her physical, makes it a priority to stay in shape, but isn't over the top with makeup and ensuring her hair looks perfect like some of the "pretty-pretty" girls may be.

In fact, that might actually turn her off, because she understands most athletic gents do want an attractive girl, but she needs to be in shape and not whiney, weak, or lack confidence in herself.

What's important here is that you just accept yourself for who you are. Consider your natural draw, tolerances and preferences, and CHOOSE to be happy with that. If you're the girl that's athletic, confident, and moderately pretty, be happy in that, and focus on being true to you. If you're happy being the skinny computer geek that hates sweating, loves numbers, electronics, hiding in the corner, and only having a handful of friends, it's critical that you are happy in that.

Experts agree, your mental can't run optimally without efficient physical function. This means regular exercise up to an hour each day. By keeping your heart and lungs pumping strong with cardiovascular exercise, and building your body lean and muscular strong with weight lifting and resistance training, you are setting your physical up to win against the challenges of life, while boosting your mental capacity.

So what if you aren't happy with your physical?

If you are honest with yourself and really aren't content with your "physical" appearance, the part of you that gets showcased to the world, then you need to stop being unhappy about yourself and make changes. Here you need to keep things in perspective though, be reasonable, and set yourself up for success.

Let's say you are a teeny-tiny nerdy type that stands at five foot and weighs under a hundred pounds. **DO NOT** expect you're going to magically transform into a 6 foot muscular football star that all the cheerleaders dream about. That's unrealistic and just not who you are. Let it go, and move on to something more achievable. Work with the factors that aren't absolute, the ones you can change.

Perhaps you want to get yourself into shape and build some muscle. Maybe you'd like to get a little more social by venturing outside of your computer-based groups and try new hobbies and interests. Joining the local gym and playing basketball or volleyball are great places to start.

You could always join a beginner biking club and take to the road. The idea is, that if you want to change your physical appearance to influence the direction you are going in life, you can. Just make certain you understand it's easier to just accept some of your traits, and embrace them because they are who you are. If you want to make changes, there's lots of "physical" you can adjust to change you for the better.

Physical changes when choosing yourself first

The physical is subjective, something that is ever-changing. Some physical changes require very little time or effort, like coloring your hair, changing your clothing style, or deciding you are going to wear jewelry. Other physical changes may require more effort and time to make them your new reality.

Maybe you want to lose a hundred pounds and get lean and fit. Or perhaps you are a scrawny little thing, and want to put on some weight to transform into sexy, hard muscle, that's going to make your wife go crazy in lust. It really doesn't matter, except whatever physical changes you make, must be done for YOU first, not someone else.

For example, maybe you have breastfed your children, and in the process lost most of your breasts. Before children you used to be a full C, and now your reality is A. By getting a boob job, this may be something that will help give you the womanly confidence you need in your life. A decision you need to make. But following through may very well support the concept of choosing yourself first. However, if you're only considering this because your partner complains all the time about the breasts you used to have, this is NOT putting yourself first, and there will only be negative energy in making such a drastic move. Does this make sense to you?

The idea with this introductory book on choosing yourself first, is to recognize what's important to you, remove the negative interference, and create your reality so you can be a better you.

YOU have life choices.

YOU have the power to determine your reality.

YOU have the ability and know-how to flip your world to positive just by using your noggin.

The physical is something that's viewed in society today as superficial, but it can't be discarded because it does influence your internal happiness. If you are happy on the inside, but trapped in an unhappy and unhealthy obese shell, it's pretty difficult to say you are choosing yourself first. This circumstance requires physical change in order to reach your true potential in happiness and life satisfaction. Wouldn't you agree?

My Thoughts . . .

Your physical appearance influences your happiness whether you like it or not. Right or wrong, people make conclusions by your appearance, and these factors can open or close doors of opportunity. What's important here, is that you make physical changes for YOU and nobody else. If you want to change your hairstyle or the clothes you wear to feel better and more positive about yourself, then do it. Losing ten pounds may be a positive for you, something that will boost your spirit.

The key is to tune into your wants, needs, desires, visions and expectations of you, and adjust accordingly. Life is always changing and never stands still. This means with an open mind and a willingness *to change, you are making the right decisions for you. Putting yourself **FIRST** is exactly what you deserve.*

Nutritional Improvement

Your body is dependent on essential nutrients in order to function optimally. Lean protein, carbohydrates, good fats, and various vitamins, minerals, and lots of water are critical to your good health. The more you're able to supply your body with these essential nutrients, the better it will function for you, and not just physically but mentally too.

Wholesome foods that aren't processed and packed full of harmful toxins, preservatives, and chemicals, are what you need to function internally without negative interference, which eventually triggers disease and illness, steals energy, and flips your positive life attitude to negative.

When it comes to losing weight, choosing yourself first is not the newest fad diet to clean your system out and drop a few pounds. Rather you owe it to yourself to make positive change that's going to help you get happier about you inside and out. Choosing to cut back on processed foods, eat plenty of fresh fruits and veggies, lean meats, healthy whole grains, and good fats sparingly, is deciding to choose yourself first.

*Balance

* Variety

* Moderation

These are all important concepts in creating healthy habits for life. Tune into your body and listen to what it's telling you. If your tummy is rumbling that means you're hungry. That's not the signal to declare victory and starve yourself more.

Adventurous eating is going to keep things exciting, because you never know unless you try. Sometimes healthy tastes take a little time to develop, but are most definitely worth it in the end.

When it comes to management, moderation is the key factor. Having too much or too little of something is stressful for your mind and body. All foods, including sweets, eaten in moderation is your best choice.

Key Factor in Creating Healthy Eating Habits to Improve YOU

Hands down, one of the most important changes you need to implement, is opening your mind to change. Change is a good thing, and the only way you're going to get different results is to physically change your habits.

Try replacing your negative eating habits with positive ones that make sense to you and are sustainable. Get that dreaded "Diet" word out of your vocabulary, because it's negative and will influence all your positive thoughts of change without optimism.

Look at your food changes as "positive lifestyle changes." Ones that are going to be permanent, and your *new* normal. With this expectation and positive drive to make it happen, it WILL become your reality, and you will accept and believe you deserve to be happy and put yourself first.

Tips for making positive nutrition changes

* One adjustment at a time. It's important not to overwhelm yourself here. Focus on changing one negative action at a time and adjusting when ready. First, you might like to switch your carbohydrate intake from simply unhealthy, nutrient poor, and often processed food choices, to healthy and wholesome complex carbohydrates. Instead of a couple pieces of white bread with butter in the morning, you might opt for whole grain toast with a smear of peanut butter. Providing your body the energy boosting carbs and muscle building protein it requires to give you pure energy that lasts.

Instead of a pastry muffin from the vending machine for your afternoon snack, you might opt for a low-fat yogurt and bowl of fresh berries. This will give your body the protein it requires for cell building, calcium for strong bones and teeth, and the protective antioxidants from the berries that will fight tooth and nail against free radicals that are looking to trigger serious disease in your body.

* Paying attention to serving size is critical in putting yourself first. Whether it's just to run "cleaner," lose weight, gain energy, or deter disease. Restaurant portions are often 2-3 times the size your body needs. Learn to listen to your body, chew slowly, and stop before you're going to explode. If you're having a serving of protein-rich nuts, that's only about 6-8 almonds. A portion of whole grain pasta is just 3/4's of a cup. Half a bagel, one slice of whole grain bread, or 3/4's a cup of BROWN rice is all you need. One cup of veggies, a cup of milk, or one piece of fruit constitutes a serving. A 2x2 inch cube of cheese, and a portion of meat about the size of a deck of cards is all your system needs in a serving.

Don't get overwhelmed here, because these portion sizes are often a shocker for most, and it'll take some adjustment time to get used to. Just keep in mind you will make this your new normal if you commit to making it your reality.

* Remove the junk food from your reach. This one is tough, but makes a huge difference when push comes to shove. If you don't have processed foods in the house, you are less likely to end up munching on them when your tummy signals hunger. It's the same sort of thing as freezing your credit card in a block of

ice to force yourself to think long and hard about using it, literally.

Changes take time, persistence, repetition, and practice. You're going to have to focus your mind on taking positive baby steps to make changes that are going to lead you to your ultimate goals. The harder you work at it, the faster and greater the results.

* A support system will help. Telling people about the positive food changes you're making and why, is only going to help you when life throws you a curve ball. Knowing you have important people in your life watching out for you and believing in you, will make the world of difference.

* Accept that you are human. You are human and you'll have missteps along the way, when making these beneficial food habit changes to put yourself first. You may eat a little too much when out with friends on occasion, or end up having a piece of cake when you weren't planning on it. Don't worry about it! Forget about it, learn from it, FORGIVE YOURSELF, and move forward positively. The last thing you want to do is beat yourself up and throw in the towel. A slip here and there will not interfere with positive progress. The only way that'll happen, is if you give up on yourself and stop believing, which of course isn't an option.

My Thoughts . . .

You are what you eat ,and your nutrition is something you can always work on. It's not about choosing foods that are "right" or "wrong" for you. The idea is to learn to focus on making better food choices, and controlling your serving size a little better. Look towards moderation and giving your body and mind a chance to adjust and accept your nutrition changes. Try not to make the mistake of taking too many steps simultaneously here, because it easily gets overwhelming, making it tough to see the silver lining. Don't let yourself lose sight of the purpose with change, and that's to put yourself first.

You are important. How you look, feel, act, and function, and this means how you fuel your body is oodles important. If you eat crap, you'll look and feel like crap, and that's not what you deserve. By taking smart steps, considering your personal preferences and tolerances to make "better" nutritional choices, you're going to take action on putting YOU first. It's the very least of which you deserve.

Emotional Wellness

Emotional healthy people are in control of their behaviors and emotions for the most part, enabling them to handle life challenges, build strong relationships, and recoup faster after life has thrown a tough curveball. This requires effort and strategy. Your emotional wellness is something that constantly needs to be worked on, and by taking steps to improve your emotional health you will reward all facets of your world. From boosting confidence and mood, to building resilience and bettering the overall enjoyment of your life. This all helps to tell yourself you deserve to come first.

What is Emotional Health?

This refers to how you're doing psychologically. Looking into factors like how you feel about you and your relationships, how you manage and deal with your feelings, and your management of obstacles, is all connected with your cognitive processing.

A few factors of people that are considered to be emotionally healthy are:

* Overall sense of happiness in life and self.

* Having a true life direction and sense of meaning and purpose.

* Experiencing an excitement for life.

* Having self-confidence and strong self-esteem.

* The ability to adapt smoothly and positively to change.

* Being able to handle stress and not focus on it.

* Balances life in work, play, sleeping and adventure.

* Having and sustaining fulfilling relationships.

Always working toward positive emotional health is going to help you be your best, putting yourself first, and gaining positive strength because of it.

Steps toward Positive Emotional Health

* Consciously focus on the positive no matter what situation you are dealing with.

* Working to acknowledge and accept what makes you happy, and make these things a life focus. If you love nature, make sure you take time out each day to enjoy something in nature. You deserve that and more.

* Open your mind to things in life that excite you and go for it. If you've thought about skydiving or going

white water rafting, then do it. If you want to travel to a far off land, and come face to face with the wild and wondrous animals that inhabit the land, then go for it. The idea is to follow your gut and set a plan in place to make it happen. If you really want to experience something you need to believe that you can and follow through.

* Set yourself up for success in life so that you build confidence and self-esteem. This will propel you to surprise yourself in everything that you CAN do.

* Learn to accept the fact life has stresses, and things aren't going to always go your way. That's okay, and what's important is that you take the time to consciously focus on the positives and deal with the stresses, but don't enable them to consume you. It doesn't take long for a mole hill to grow into a mountain, and that makes it pretty tough to see the sunshine in yourself or life.

* Life is all about balance, and putting yourself first means you are always striving to get your work, play, adventure, and rest equal. Of course it's pretty tough to make this happen, but you can make a conscious effort to look for balance. If you're working too much, book a vacation. If you are finding that your sleep is being neglected, then cut back on your late night activities so you can get a few more zzz's in. It's important to check yourself at the door regularly, and make adjustments where needed.

* Having healthy relationships is important for emotional wellbeing. This is something you need to work on continuously. Being able to communicate

with others on various levels is critical in the game of life.

Emotional Red Flags

* Having trouble sleeping

* Feeling low or hopeless all the time

* Trouble concentrating

* Turning to drugs and alcohol

* Death or thoughts of suicide

* Uncontrollable fears, thoughts of self-destruction

If you are experiencing these symptoms it's important you speak with a professional.

My Thoughts . . .

Various internal and external factors are integral in shaping your emotional health, and there's always room to adjust your psychological wellbeing. By choosing yourself first, you need to pay attention to your emotional, which is directly related to your internal happiness. Your emotions can't physiologically work with your logical, but they do influence one another, and an emotionally healthier you IS putting YOU first.

Elite Social

Social skills are necessary to interact and communicate with people verbally and otherwise, suggesting your thoughts and feelings through body language, gestures, and how you look.

We are social creatures, and over time have created various platforms in which to communicate our thoughts, feelings, and desires with others. It's how we say things, what we say, the words used, and manner in which the message is delivered that communicates to people.

Improving your social skills is making a conscious effort to put yourself first, with the goal of improving your life in all areas.

Advantages with Elite Social Skills

Deeper and Meaningful Relationships - If you are able to connect and relate to others with ease, the chances are good you'll have more meaningful relationships. People want to feel heard, understood and appreciated, just as you do. Without interpersonal relationships it's pretty tough to advance forward in life. Another advantage is, experts believe people that are socially "well" have a lot less negatives in their lives.

Improved Communication - Those with better social skills seem to communicate better with people, and this means they can efficiently and effectively get what they want faster, making them feel more valued and successful.

Faster Career Advancement - Studies have proven people with better social skills advance up the corporate ladder much faster. This makes sense, because a positive social person is much more appealing to work with, and more open to opportunity than a quiet shy individual.

More Overall Happiness - Professionals agree, people that are the center of attention socially tend to be happier as individuals overall. This is because an intrinsic need of humans is to feel loved, respected, wanted, needed and appreciated. Socially elite people get all of this and this propels them to greatness.

Tips to Improve Your Social

LISTEN

This skill may be the most unappreciated social skill out there. Naturally our egos want us to have the center of attention on ourselves, making it easy to forget to listen. If someone feels they aren't being heard, this throws a wrench into the smooth positive communication we strive for.

Take Action . . .

By making the conscious choice to forget about yourself and focus externally on the person you are communicating with, you are teaching yourself to step out of the spotlight. It doesn't have to always be about you, and with persistence and recognition you can teach your ego this. Help you find that "balance" we all strive for in life.

PRACTICE BEING INTERESTED IN OTHER PEOPLE

By making the effort to be interested in others, you'll improve your listening skills, and help round yourself out. Actually becoming interested in what people are thinking and feeling will help you see another side of them that's often quite different than you initially thought. This "learned" focus will also help improve internal connections you have with everyone.

Take Action . . .

When people feel they are being heard, they're naturally more receptive towards you, willingly opening the door of opportunity for you to walk through.

RELAX WHEN CRITICIZED

This one can be very difficult, especially for those of us that are extremely sensitive to others, some of which is a reflection of your personality, and can only be swayed so much.

You shouldn't just ignore critical remarks, because they may hold merit. If so, you can use them to improve yourself, or perhaps how you are reacting to a specific situation. It's key to remind yourself that criticism is most often reflective of how another person is feeling, and really has nothing to do with you, as weird and twisted as that may sound.

Perhaps this person is just jealous of your accomplishments, has hormonal issues because of their period, or just woke up on the wrong side of the bed. What you need to keep crystal clear in your mind, is that you only control yourself and nobody else. By flipping your thought process and taming your ego, you'll see the situation from the other side of the fence, diminishing your need to react negatively. In other words, you may even empathize with the person, and think about ways to make them feel better. The focus won't be on the fact they were criticizing you. It's all about conscious perspective.

Take Action . . .

Don't let others influence you negatively, even when throwing out criticism. Try putting yourself in their shoes first, and use what they are saying positively instead of taking it directly to heart. Most certainly don't avoid doing something for fear of what others may think. This is just inhibiting yourself, and handing the control and direction of YOUR life over to someone else. This just doesn't make sense any way you look at it. If you choose yourself first, it's very important you relax and never let criticism take you down.

TREAT OTHER PEOPLE AS YOU WANT TO BE TREATED

I know you've heard this phrase before, and it's a great one to live by. Everything comes back around, and by making it habit to treat others with love, attention, and respect, for the most part, this is what you will receive back. Will there be exceptions to the rules? Of course, but two wrongs don't make a right. By doing the "right" thing you may even sway those who choose to live by their ego, to change their tune at some point, or at least think about it. It's worth a shot don't you think?

Take Action . . .

Look in the mirror and tell me what you see. This reflection holds the key to what you will receive back in life. You will make mistakes and wish from time to time you could reverse the clock, but as long as you focus on treating others the way you'd like to be treated, you're putting yourself first.

With a positive attitude and kind words, you will make life that much more for yourself and everyone around you. It's worth a few minutes of thought don't you think?

POSITIVE THINKING AND ACTION

Make it a habit of running from the negative towards the positive to make you a better you. This doesn't mean you don't pay any attention to it, but it's important you learn how to not focus on it or interfere with your life daily.

Negativity has a way to pull you under and eat you up before you know it. Experts agree, the successful people in life for the most part surround them with positivity. This means in their environment, relationships, attitude, actions, and words. By focusing on the positive in everything you do, even the crappy stuff, you will choose yourself first.

Life is full of challenges both good and bad, and you have the power to make the good stuff fabulous and the bad stuff better. The mind is a powerful thing.

Take Action . . .

It all starts with a decision to look for the positive and run from the negative, to consciously push the negativity aside so you can make room for the positive. It's not easy, but with a little practice you will find the sun shining a little brighter each day and this is something you deserve.

ZIP IT FROM TIME TO TIME

By learning silence you are freeing your ears to listen. We've all put our foot in our mouth on occasion, and by recognizing when we should be quiet there will be fewer times you wish you could reverse. There are extremes here, because keeping everything inside is not healthy either. It's all about balance, and sometimes this requires silence.

Take Action . . .

By calmly staying silent, a whole lot of negatives can be avoided. Maybe you want to practice counting down from ten before you comment in a heated discussion. If you disagree with a situation at work, it's important to know when to silence yourself, sleep on it, and see if you have the same feelings in the morning. It's much easier just not to say anything than to try and erase something you've said.

DON'T JUST USE WORDS

Words are just one way we communicate with others. Your tone, choice of words, and body language are also effective methods to get your thoughts, feelings, and perspective across. Eye contact, the way you hold your head, and hand placement are just a few tools that help with communication.

Take Action . . .

Practice being aware of all the tools your body possesses that will help you positively communicate. Use them to help remove negative interference and better your social skills as a whole. Choosing yourself first is all about caring. This requires constant effort in making positive change with yourself. You are worth the effort.

My Thoughts . . .

Your social abilities are truly reflective of your character, who you are, how efficiently you function, where you're headed in life, and whether you are traveling with a smile or frown. Your social skills are something that can always be improved to make you happier and more productive. Putting yourself first does take effort and know-how. The ball's in your court here. Are you going to shoot or just not bother?

Sound Spiritual

By spiritual, I am not referring specifically to religious beliefs. For some, this is a part of it, but it's not an absolute.

Spiritualism is a search for something sacred, and can be achieved or satiated through religion, yoga, meditation, positive thought, or just personalized reflection. In most instances, paying attention to the spiritual is beneficial, and touches all aspects of life.

Numerous studies have been conducted and here are a few positive traits of spiritual people:

* **Compassion is heightened** - People of spiritual nature have a strong belief in compassion. They are

more likely to show empathy and look at life through positive thought.

* Spiritual people are more likely to be thankful - Experts agree, showing gratitude encourages positive emotion. These people are more generous, understanding, and forgiving to start. It's all key in choosing yourself first.

* Increase awareness of self - People that incorporate spiritualism in their life are open to personal growth, and striving towards goals. They are focused on positive internal traits, and utilize these positive characteristics to improve all aspects of life.

* Spiritual people succeed - Positive spirit is scientifically linked to success in relationships, work, and life in general. These people tend to see meaning in everything, are optimistic, and just don't give up.

* Take time to smell and appreciate the flowers - Spiritual people are more likely to take time out of their day to reflect on what's around them, and use this information positively. In other words, they take the time required to process and make better, or more informed life decisions in general. Finding pleasure in the smaller things in life is a highlight of their day.

So how can you improve your spiritual health?

If you feel like you are missing something in life, maybe you are drained or you just don't feel that you are getting everything you need, a moment to reflect on your spiritual is in order.

* Choose to be positive - You are in control of you, and consciously choosing to focus on the positive is going to shove the negative off the stage. When you are stuck in a negative rut, it's really tough to see anything but negative. You lose your ability to keep perspective, and studies show that negative thought in general generates even more negative, even in positive scenarios.

*** Remove yourself from the situation** - If you're feeling frustrated, drained or down, the first thing you need to do is recognize this and remove yourself. A change of scenery does wonders for a negative mood or "moment." Maybe you just need to get up from behind your desk and go for a walk, or just take a break to read a good book or take a calm bath. Your spirit needs a break from time to time, and putting a little positivity in your day does wonders for you and your positive spirit.

*** Recognize and fuel your passion** - It's important you do what makes you happy, and making sure you focus and fuel your passion, is showing your "self" you care. Choosing yourself first, means you make certain you take the time to enjoy things you love. This is only going to feed your positive inner spirit, boosting you up to higher levels of achievement in love and life.

*** Accept sadness** - Life isn't all about rainbows and cotton candy clouds. There is sadness, devastation, and loss in life that is a reality. By learning to accept a sad situation and move past it in time, you are strengthening your spirit from within, and this is making you a stronger person overall.

* **Be open and willing** - With an open mind comes an open heart, and this means you are always looking to build yourself bigger and stronger inside and out. New experiences are keeping your life perspective fresh and live, fueling the passion from within. Opening your mind, body, and soul, to all this fabulous world has to offer to better you.

My Thoughts . . .

Your spirit is a direct reflection of "the real" you. You can't hide behind your spirit, nor should you want to. By making positive choices in life, and opening your whole self to new opportunity, you're making the conscious decision that you are worth it. For that, you deserve to reach that ultimately higher level of happiness. This only proves that you come first.

Final Thoughts . . . Better Life, Better You

The first thing you should do is accept and love yourself for who you are. This is the first step in putting yourself first. You see, this isn't a singular thing here. There's not just one action you should or shouldn't do to improve yourself. There are hundreds of factors involved, and this means opening your perspective to slow down a minute and take a look at the big picture, is extremely critical.

* The mental is key because if your thoughts aren't positive and productive, it's very difficult for you to progress forward and reach goals you never thought

possible. Positive thinking is the key here, and it's not natural but learned. By consciously practicing positive perspective, you will in time incorporate this powerful means of thinking into your being, and then you will begin reaping the rewards.

* The physical is critical because if you aren't physically able to handle the curveballs of life, how can you expect to be happy and healthy? Prevention and exceptance of yourself are two points that need focus and understanding. Working to build your body and set your mind positive. Let's have no whining here. Either dig deep and make those changes, or shut up, accept, and get happy.

* How you fuel your vehicle is critical in the game of life. If you want to go through life full of energy and wellness, then you need to communicate this to your body by fueling it nutritiously. Avoid processed foods loaded with fat, high calories, and little nutrition. Choose instead to eat plenty of protective antioxidant rich fresh fruits and veggies, lean meats that provide protein for sound cell building, complex carbohydrates for longer term energy, and unsaturated healthy fats that will provide energy and keep your thinking sharp and precise. You are what you eat rings true here. Perfect is not what we are looking for, just "better."

* Your emotional health is an important feature in choosing yourself first. Emotions are reflective of how your process information and deal with situations both positive and negative. Learning how to transform your emotions into a positive reflection is hugely beneficial

in your overall health strength. Understanding this takes time, persistence, and continuous practical monitoring. Your emotional well being is something that can only get better, but first you have to choose to believe and act on this.

* We are internally built to socialize, and this means that social interaction is critical in your wellbeing. Studies show, people that lack social relations develop all sorts of mental issues, and often end up sick and diseased over time. That's how important your social is. Working to better your social skills is a signal that you care about yourself, and are willing to work towards making yourself better. Improving your communication skills is only going to help boost your internal character, confidence, belief, and perception of you all tainted positive. If you want it, go get it!

* The spiritual is often misunderstood because people connect it with a religion or god. In basic, it's a belief you strive for, one that has no ceiling, and can always grow deeper with attention and time. Your spirit is a part of who you are, and what you will become. It's the key to transformation on a higher level than just improving your mental, emotional, and physical function for example. Take the time to step outside of yourself and tune into your spirit. Nurture and build it, and there's no doubt you are choosing yourself first.

You are important, along with every day of your life. You can choose to watch it pass buy and "wish" your life away, or you can decide to make the most of the world around you. It's up to you to **choose yourself first**, and take control of your reality. Make the choice to want better, more positive, and crazy exciting.

You control you, your decisions and life path, nobody else. Time to take action, and choosing yourself first is the first step in a positive forever - believe it!

Last Thoughts…

*THANK-YOU for reading my masterpiece. I hope you learned a little something, or at least got a few smiles.

*I would appreciate a millisecond or three of your time for a quick review, to help me build my masterful book empire higher.

*Whatever you do,don't forget to smile, and of course, check out my website for more of my e-Book masterpieces at: www.flawlesscreativewriting.com

Cathy☺

Disclaimer

All Rights Reserved Copyright © 2014 Cathy Wilson

No part of this book can be reproduced, stored, or transmitted by any means including recording, scanning, photocopying, electronic or print without written permission from the author.

While utmost care has been taken to ensure accuracy of the written content, the readers are advised to follow the guidelines and ideas mentioned herein at their own risk. The author in no case shall be responsible for any personal or commercial damage that results due to misinterpretation of information.

This book does not take personal situations into consideration, and therefore may not be fit for every purpose. All readers are encouraged to seek professional advice for a specific situation.